BETTER WAY BOOKS

Slim your Hips

ISBN: 0-88176-316-0

Cover Design: Jeff Hapner
Illustrations: Len Martinez

Printed in Canada

CONTENTS

THE 7 DAY PROGRAM

Looking sleek, trim, and healthy—that's your goal. Slim hips and thighs are essential to that lean look. Yet the most common figure complaints are in that area from the waist to the knees. These figure problems are usually caused not only by excess fat. They are also caused by muscles that are out of shape. The muscles in this part of the body are important in several ways. They affect your energy level and your posture, as well as your figure. When these muscles are out of shape, you suffer threefold.

This 7 day program to Slim Your Hips is specifically designed to firm up those muscles. No matter what shape you're in now, you can look and feel better—much sooner than you think.

You may have tried to diet off your extra inches. Paying attention to what you eat is, of course, essential to your health, fitness, and figure. But weight loss alone will not give you the firm, shapely figure you want. You need well-toned muscles to have a good figure. That's why you need a regular, carefully planned exercise program.

The Slim Your Hips program gives you an exercise plan for every day of the week. Each exercise routine takes only about 30 minutes. The exercises are foolproof and easy to follow. The entire program has been designed to produce balanced muscle development and shaping, while avoiding injury and soreness. Follow this simple program, exercising regularly and vigorously each day. You'll feel slimmer, firmer, stronger—not just in your hips and thighs, but all over your body.

If you really want the figure you've always dreamed of, get this book out every day. Put on some fast-paced music to swing you along. You'll soon notice that you're looking a little better every day you exercise. It will take some effort, but it will all be worth it. Don't expect overnight results. But within only a few weeks, this program can change your figure dramatically. It can shape you up enough to make people say, "Gee, you look great."

Following the program

The new Slim Your Hips program offers 7 new exercise routines—a different routine for every day of the week. During the first 6 days, the program alternates days of lighter exercise with days of more vigorous exercise, as recommended by medical experts on physical fitness. At the same time, the exercises gradually progress from Day 1 on, so that Day 6 is the most vigorous—and most beneficial—routine of the week. Day 7 is a maintenance-level routine. You might want to arrange your weekly exercise program so that you do the Day 7 routine when you may have less time or energy to devote to exercise, perhaps on the weekend.

Each of the 7 new routines includes warm-up exercises, spot exercises for the hips and thighs, stretches for flexibility, and cool-down exercises.

Most fitness experts agree that each type of exercise serves an important purpose. Each is essential to a sound fitness program.

Warm ups get your body going. They generally loosen up the muscles all over your body and get your heart and lungs working at higher levels. Warm ups are essential for two main reasons.

When your body is properly warmed up, the more vigorous hip and thigh exercises are more effective. Warm ups raise the body and muscle temperature to efficient levels. They increase the blood supply in the muscles and increase the rate and force of muscle contractions. Your car works more efficiently after the engine is warmed up. The same is true for your body.

Warm ups also make you less prone to injury when you go on to more vigorous exercises. They stretch the ligaments and tissues to permit greater flexibility. By gradually activating muscle fibers, you'll help prevent muscle tears and sprains. How will you know when you've warmed up enough? You'll be slightly out of breath, and you'll break the sweat barrier.

The exercises for the hips and thighs are a combination of spot exercises and stretches. Our *spot exercises* are muscle-toners, not "spot reducers." Exercising one area of the body will not reduce the amount of fat in that area. However, our spot exercises can change the shape of an area. Restoring muscle tone makes the hips and thighs firmer and more attractively shaped.

Stretches are often included as the last step in an exercise. Stretches help avoid injury by increasing flexibility and range of movement. The connective tissues of your body are like rubber bands. If not stretched frequently, the tissues become tight and limit your movement. If not stretched at all for a long time, the tissues may snap, causing injury and pain. Take the stretches slowly at first. Do not stretch any farther than you feel comfortable. As the ligaments gradually loosen, your stretches will gofarther.

The hip and thigh exercises are carefully designed to help your muscles develop evenly. This even development of all the hip and thigh muscles is what gives you the shape and proportion you're after. Our exercise routines carefully alternate the muscles exercised. One exercise may work on the front of the leg; the next, on the back of the leg. One may work on the inside of the thigh; the next, on the outside. That is one more reason to do all the exercises in each routine in the order given.

Cool downs are exercises that allow your body to slow down gradually. After strenuous work, the body must readjust to pre-exercise levels of function. Cool downs help your muscles begin to relax. They allow your circulatory system to slow down gradually. If you stop exercising suddenly, without this tapering-off period, blood collects in the muscles and veins. This could cause dizziness and weakness. A proper cool down also helps minimize stiffness and soreness.

Making it work

To get the most from the time and energy you put into this program, keep these guidelines in mind.

● Wear comfortable clothing that allows you to move freely, such as shorts, a leotard, or a light exercise suit.

● Exercise in tennis shoes, in socks, or barefoot—whatever is most comfortable to you. If you have a weak back, weak knees, or weak ankles, wear tennis shoes or running shoes. You may sometimes need to remove shoes, however, for exercises that require sliding the feet on the floor.

● If possible, exercise on a wooden floor or on a carpet. Exercising on concrete surfaces can be hard on your body. For floor exercises, try to work on a mat, a carpet remnant, a piece of foam rubber, or a folded towel.

● When doing chair exercises, use a sturdy chair with a firm base. Be sure the chair is strong enough to support your weight. As an extra caution, place the chair under a table to prevent its tipping over. You may also lean on a windowsill or a kitchen counter, instead of a chair, for these exercises.

● Try to exercise every day, or at least four times a week. A regular exercise program offers the most benefit for your body.
● Establish your own exercise schedule. You shouldn't exercise just before bedtime or just after you eat. Most any other time is fine. Once you choose the best time, stick to it. Exercising at the same time every day helps you develop the exercise habit.

● Follow the routines carefully. If you follow directions, you should tone and shape muscles properly, avoid injury, and suffer a minimum of soreness.

● If you cannot do an exercise exactly as it is described, don't worry. Try it, and then go on to the next exercise. Don't feel discouraged. As you increase your strength and flexibility, you will eventually be able to do most of the exercises. Then you will realize just how far you have progressed.

● Remember that your individual body structure may make an exercise difficult for you. Body structure and flexibility vary greatly from person to person. The structure of your joints or the length of your arms or legs may prevent you from doing an exercise exactly as it is described. Don't push yourself past your own body's limits. Aim toward what is asked for in each exercise, doing the best that you can.

● Do the number of repetitions given in the text, until the exercises are easy for you. Then gradually increase the number of repetitions for each exercise. For some exercises, the text recommends the number of repetitions you should try to work toward. In general, you might aim toward eventually doubling the repetitions given in the text. But don't try to go too far too fast. Don't try to double the repetitions all at once. Add only 3 to 5 repetitions at a time, until that number becomes easy.

● At the end of each day's exercises, you should feel a healthy, relaxed sense of fatigue. Exercise that does not tax the body does not help the body.

● No matter how rushed you may be, do not neglect to do the warm ups and cool downs. These exercises are essential for keeping your body flexible, getting your heart and lungs working efficiently, and avoiding injury and stiffness.

● As you work through each day's routine, keep your body moving. You lose some of the benefits if you take long breaks between exercises. Exercising to lively music can help you pace yourself and really keep you going.

● Learn to listen to your own body for signs of fatigue. You want to exercise vigorously enough to work up a sweat. But be careful not to overdo. If you're winded and breathless, or if you suffer sprains or stitches in the side, assume that you're exercising too vigorously. Slow down a little.

- If you haven't exercised for a while, it is normal to be a little sore and stiff when you first start. Stiffness does not mean you should stop moving. In most cases, it means you should get going again. Remember that warming up and cooling down properly will help minimize soreness.

- If you think you may be injured, stop using the injured limb. Continuing to exercise could worsen the injury. Stop your exercise program until the injury no longer hurts when you are at rest. Then gradually begin to exercise slowly and carefully.

- If you have a weak back, weak ankles, or weak knees, be careful doing exercises that put stress on those parts of the body. Those exercises will eventually strengthen the muscles in those areas. But go slowly until you build up that strength.

- Supplement this program with as much activity as possible. You should consciously aim at becoming a more physically active person. Try to do more walking, bicycling, dancing. Take the stairs instead of the elevator. Participate in whatever active sports you enjoy. Keep that energy level up.

- Don't be discouraged if you gain a little weight after the first week of exercise. A small weight gain means that the muscles are becoming firmer and denser. Those few extra pounds will disappear after another week of regular exercise.

- If you miss a week or more on this program, start again with the number of repetitions given in the text. You'll have to rebuild your strength and flexibility before increasing the number of repetitions again.

- All the exercises in this program were developed in consultation with medical experts. However, it is recommended that you consult your doctor before beginning this or any program of exercise.

Let's get going

Now you're ready to begin. You have the ground rules. You understand how this terrific program works. So get into some comfortable clothes, put some upbeat music on the stereo, and let's get moving. Remember, the hips and thighs are quick to respond to a well-designed exercise program. You could feel better and start looking firmer and slimmer by next week!

Starting position

a

b   c

WARM UP   REACH AND RUN

Assume starting position.

   a Slowly run in place, lifting the knees and landing lightly on the feet. While running, reach one arm then the other straight upward. Alternate arms with each step. Reach and run for 40 counts.

   b Bend the knees and round the back over until hands dangle at the ankles. Hold 5 counts. To return to upright position, slowly press the hips forward, straighten the legs, uncurl the back, and raise the head.

   c Raise the shoulders as high as possible. Hold 5 counts. Lower. Raise and lower shoulders twice.

Starting position

a

b

WARM UP SWING AND CIRCLE

Assume starting position.

a Kick right leg out to the side and return to center. Landing on right foot, kick left leg out to the side and return. While kicking side to side, circle arms up overhead, around, down, and up again. Kick side to side 20 times.

b Pull knee to chest. Hold for 5 counts, while slowly pressing the nose to the knee. Lower leg to floor. Repeat 3 times with each leg.

Starting position

a

SUPER SWING

Assume starting position.

a Lunge to the right, leaning over bent right knee, swinging arms overhead to the right.

b Pushing off the right foot, cross right leg up behind the left leg. At the same time, swing arms down, across, and up to the left. Lunge and kick up 4 times with each leg. Work up to 8 times each leg.

c Assume the lunge position with right knee bent. Place right hand on the floor by the right foot. Hold left ankle with the left hand. Slowly straighten the right leg as much as possible. Hold for 5 counts. Relax. Repeat 3 times to each side.

Starting position

a

b

CONTOUR SIT

Assume starting position.

   a Slowly bend knees, lowering the hips, keeping the back straight. Swing arms down toward the ankles. Continue swinging arms forward and up, straightening legs to return to an upright position. Repeat 10 times. Use the legs (not the back) to lower and raise the body.

   b Bend knees and place fingertips on the floor in front of the feet. Lift toes. Pivoting on the heels, slowly turn toes out to the sides and in again. Repeat 8 times.

*Starting
position*

a

b

KNEE PRESS I

Assume starting position.

    a Keeping the back straight, pull the knees in, swinging arms to the front. Return knees and arms to starting position. Repeat 8 times. Do not lower hips below the knees.

    b Stand. Bend left leg back. Grasp ankle with the left hand. Pull the ankle up as far as possible. Do once with each leg.

Starting position

a

b

THIGH TRIMMER

Assume starting position.

   a   Lean torso back. Touch the right
hand to the floor by the right foot. Return to
starting position. Repeat with the left hand.
Touch right hand then left hand 4 times. Work
up to 8 times.

   b   Keeping torso straight, lean back to
place both hands on the floor. Hold and stretch
for 3 counts. Push off the floor with both hands
to return to starting position. Repeat 3 times.

Starting position

a

SWING OUT

Assume starting position.

    a Swing right leg forward, trying to touch the right elbow to the right knee. Return to starting position. Repeat 10 times with each leg.

    b Rest for 5 counts. In starting position, bend the right knee. Grasp the foot with the right hand. Slowly try to straighten the leg. Then lift the leg as high as possible. Repeat 3 times with each leg.

Starting position

a

COOL DOWN SCISSORS STRETCH

Assume starting position.

a Lower left leg toward the floor, while bringing right leg toward the head. Then reverse leg positions, bringing left leg toward the head, right leg toward the floor. Repeat 30 times.

b Grasp left foot with both hands. Slowly try to straighten the leg. Hold for 5 counts. Do once with each leg.

Starting position

a

COOL DOWN   HIP HOORAY

Assume starting position.

   a Lift hips off the floor as high as possible. Hold for 5 counts.

   b Keeping hips off the floor, lift the right leg toward the head as far as possible. Hold for 5 counts. Return leg to the floor. Do once with each leg.

29

*Starting
position*

a

b

WARM UP   HEEL-TOE JIG

Assume starting position.

a   Hop on left foot, touching right heel to floor. Twist torso to the right, keeping arms to the left.

b   Hop on left foot again, touching right toe to the floor. Twist torso to the left, swinging arms to the right. Heel and toe, swinging arms back and forth, 20 times with each foot. Gradually work up to 35 times with each foot.

Starting position

a

WARM UP   THE CHEERLEADER

Assume starting position.

   a   Hop on left foot, touching right foot to floor out to the side. Swing right arm out to the side.

   b   Jump, feet together, and clap hands.

   c   Hop on right foot, touching left foot to floor out to the side. Swing left arm out to the side. Return to jump and clap. Repeat 16 times.

Starting position

a

b

THE KICKER

Assume starting position.

a Push off the left foot, shifting weight to the right leg. Kick the left leg as high as possible, touching hands to the ankle. Do 4 times with each leg. Repeat this sequence 3 times.

b In starting position, place hands on the floor, one on each side of the front leg. Very slowly slide the front leg forward as far as is comfortable. Do once with each leg.

Starting position

a

DOUBLE DIP

Assume starting position.

a Bending the left knee, bring right elbow down to the knee. Return to starting position.

b Bending knee again, bring elbow down to the calf. Return to starting position. Alternate bringing the elbow to the knee then to the calf. Repeat 8 times on each side.

c Bend left knee. Extend right leg straight back, toe on the floor. Place hands on left knee. Hold for 10 counts. Then lift and lower the hips 5 times. Repeat to the right side.

Starting position

a

KNEE PRESS II

Assume starting position.

a Holding outside of ankles, pull the knees in toward each other. Then press knees out. Repeat 8 times. Work up to 16 times. Do not lower hips below the knees.

b Place right hand on the floor. Bend right leg back. Grasp right foot with left hand. Pull the leg up and away from the body. Hold 5 counts. Do once with each leg.

*Starting
position*

a

THE CURTSY

Assume starting position.

a Swinging arms out to sides, cross left leg behind the right. Left foot on the floor, both knees bent, slowly press the left knee down toward the right calf. Hold 5 counts. Return to starting position. Repeat 8 times with each leg.

b Do the same movement, but try to touch the knee to the floor. Turn the palms up. Hold 5 counts. Return to starting position. Repeat 5 times with each leg. If you have weak knees, do not touch knee to the floor or bend knee too low.

Starting position

a

b

THE TIGHTENER

Assume starting position.

a Bend elbows down toward the floor. Then straighten the arms. Repeat 8 times. As you build strength, try to place elbows on the floor.

b Do the same exercise with the toes up, weight on the heels. Repeat 8 times.

Starting position

a

COOL DOWN   RAG DOLL

Assume starting position.

a Bending knees, swing arms down between the legs, bending forward from the waist. Swing back up to starting position. Repeat 5 times.

44

Starting position

a

COOL DOWN THE SWINGER

Assume starting position.

    a Swing arms up to the right, straightening legs and turning torso to the right. Stretch. Return to starting position. Repeat to the left side. Swing right then left 10 times.

Starting position

a

WARM UP DIXIE SHUFFLE I

Assume starting position.

a Hop on left foot, touching right foot to the floor in front of the left foot.

b Hop on left foot again, touching right foot to the floor at the right side. While touching foot left and right, move hands in small circles. Touch left and right 15 times with each foot.

c Place hands on bent knees. Lift the shoulders. Hold for 5 counts. Lower shoulders. Repeat 3 times. Slowly uncurl the back to return to an upright position.

Starting position

a

b

WARM UP   DIXIE SHUFFLE II

Assume starting position.

a Hop on left foot, touching right toe to floor at the right side. Turn torso to the right, arms right. Jump, feet together, swinging arms down. Then hip on right foot, touching left toe to the floor at the left side. Swing arms and torso to the left. Return to jump, arms down. Repeat 20 times.

b Stand with feet together, hands on bent knees. Press knees out to the sides. Hold 5 counts. Bring knees together. Repeat 3 times.

Starting position

a

THE ROCKER

Assume starting position.

   a   Keeping heels on the floor, rock the knees side to side. Swing the arms side to side at the same time. Rock knees left and right 20 times.

   b   With right knee bent, extend the left leg with the toes up. Lowering hips, try to touch hands to the floor, one hand on each side of the left foot. Hold 5 counts. Repeat with right leg extended. Do once with each leg.

Starting position

a

b

THE LITTLE DIPPER

Assume starting position.

a Keep right hand on floor in front of left foot, left hand on knee to support the back. Bending left knee lower, bend the right elbow down toward the floor. Then straighten the elbow and straighten left leg as much as possible. Repeat 10 times to each side.

b Place feet wide apart, knees slightly bent. Put hands on the floor, head down. Slide feet out as wide as possible. Then pull feet in toward each other. Repeat 5 times. Remove shoes to slide feet more easily on the floor.

Starting position

a

b

KNEE LIFTER

Assume starting position.

   a   Lift knees off the floor about 12 inches. Then lower knees to about 2 inches off the floor. Repeat 10 times without returning knees to the floor.

   b   From starting position, lift knees off the floor. Straighten the legs as much as possible. Try to press the heels back toward the floor. Return to starting position. Repeat 10 times.

Starting position

a

c

THE BIG DIPPER

Assume starting position.

a Keep left hand behind the right heel, right hand on knee to support the back. Bending right knee lower, bend the left elbow down toward the floor. Then straighten the elbow and straighten right leg as much a possible. Repeat 10 times to each side.

b Put hands on the floor, head down. Place feet wide apart, weight on the heels with the toes up. Slide heels out as wide as possible. Then pull heels in toward each other. Repeat 5 times. Remove shoes to slide feet more easily on the floor.

Starting position

a

b

CROSS KICK

Assume starting position.

    a Raise right leg up to the side as high as possible. Touch toes with the right hand.

    b Lower the leg, crossing to touch the floor in front of the left leg. Return to starting position. Repeat 15 times with each leg.

Starting position

a

b

COOL DOWN   GET YOUR KICKS

Assume starting position.

a Alternately kick right leg then left leg straight up for 5 counts. Alternately kick left leg and right leg forward for 5 counts. Repeat, kicking up then forward, 20 times.

b Lower legs to the floor. Place the hands at the sides, palms down. Lift the hips off the floor. Hold 5 counts. Lower hips. Repeat 3 times.

Starting position

a

b

COOL DOWN   THE EXTENDER

Assume starting position.

a Lifting feet off the floor, bend knees in toward the chest. Then extend both legs straight up.

b Bend knees in toward the chest again. Then extend legs forward. Repeat the sequence (knees to chest, legs up, knees to chest, legs forward) 20 times.

61

Starting position

a

WARM UP DO   THE TWIST

Assume starting position.

a   With feet slightly apart, twist the body left then right, pivoting on the balls of the feet. Swing the arms side to side at the same time. Twist right and left 10 times.

b   Now bend the knees and hips lower. Twist right and left 5 times. Repeat the sequence (twisting 10 times upright, 5 times bent low) 3 times.

***Starting
position***

a

b

WARM UP   LET'S TWIST AGAIN

Assume starting position.

a   Keep feet wide apart. Lean body to the left. Twist for 5 counts, pivoting on the balls of the feet. Swing the arms back and forth at the same time. Now lean to the right and twist for 5 counts. Repeat the sequence (twisting 5 counts leaning left, 5 counts leaning right) 3 times.

b   Stand, weight on the left leg. Pull the right leg up, holding the foot with both hands. Press the foot away from the body. Hold for 5 counts. Do once with each leg.

Starting position

a

b

KNEE PULL-UP

Assume starting position.

a Keep the left knee bent. Lift the right foot off the floor, bringing the knee up toward the chest. At the same time, cross the arms in front of the chest. Return to starting position. Repeat 10 times with each leg.

b Stand with feet together, legs straight. Slowly bend forward. Place the hands behind the knees. Pull the head down toward the knees. Hold for 5 counts. Relax. Repeat 3 times.

Starting position

a

b

PERFECTION PULL

Assume starting position.

a Keep the left knee bent, hands on the ankle. Lift the right foot off the floor and bring the knee up toward the chest. Return to starting position. Repeat 15 times with each leg.

b Stand with feet wide apart, legs straight. Slowly bend forward. Place the hands behind the knees. Pull the head down toward the knees. Hold for 5 counts. Relax. Repeat 3 times.

*Starting
position*

a

b

HIP, HIP AWAY

Assume starting position.

    a Lift the right foot off the floor, bringing the knee up toward the chest. Return to starting position. Repeat 10 times with each leg.

    b Stand, weight on left leg. Lift the right leg, placing right hand on the inside of the foot. Extend the leg up to the side. Straighten the leg as much as possible. Hold for 3 counts. Do once with each leg.

Starting position

a

THE THIGH SHAPER

Assume starting position.

    a Lift the left heel, keeping toes on the floor. Return heel to floor. Repeat with right heel. Alternate lifting left heel then right heel 20 times.

    b Rest for 10 counts. Now lift and lower both heels at the same time. Repeat 20 times.

Starting position

a

b

LIFT AND CIRCLE

Assume starting position.

a Raise the right leg up to the side as high as possible.

b Lower right leg so it is parallel to the floor. Then move the leg in a large circle to the side. Return to starting position. Repeat (lifting up, then circling) 5 times with the right leg, 5 times with the left leg. Repeat the sequence 3 times.

Starting position

a

b

COOL DOWN KICK OUT

Assume starting position.

a Holding the back of a chair, lift the left knee up toward the chest. Then extend the left leg out in back. Repeat, bringing knee to chest and extending leg, 10 times with each leg.

b Place right foot on the seat of the chair. Bend the left knee. Slowly reach hands to right ankle. Hold 5 counts. Do once with each leg.

77

Starting position

a

b

COOL DOWN THE PENDULUM

Assume starting position.

a Keep hands on the back of a chair. Swing the right leg across the body to the left side. Then swing the leg across to the right side. Raise the leg as high as possible. Swing each leg side to side 15 times. Be careful not to hit the toes on the chair as you swing across.

b Place the right foot on the seat of the chair. Keep both legs straight. Slowly reach hands to the right ankle. Hold for 5 counts. Do once with each leg.

Starting position

a

WARM UP   CHORUS LINE I

Assume starting position.

a Hop on the left foot, touching the right foot to the floor behind the left foot. At the same time, cross the arms in front of the chest. Hop on the left foot again, returning the right foot and the arms to starting position. Repeat 20 times with each foot.

Starting position

a

b

WARM UP   CHORUS LINE II

Assume starting position.

a   Hop on the left foot, kicking the right foot out to the side, swinging the arms down toward the right leg. Jump, feet together. Then hop on the right foot, kicking the left foot out to the side, swinging arms down toward the left leg. Return to jump in the center. Repeat 20 times.

b   Bring the right knee up to the chest, arms encircling the leg, hands holding the elbows. Slowly raise the leg as high as possible. Hold 5 counts. Do once with each leg.

Starting position

a

THE DONKEY

Assume starting position.

a Keep fingertips on the floor. Bend the left knee in toward the chest.

b Then extend the leg directly to the side. Try to extend the leg at the height of the hip.

c Bend the knee in to the chest again. Extend the leg, straight back. Repeat (knee in, leg to side, knee in, leg back) 10 times with each leg. Gradually work up to 20 times with each leg.

Starting position

a

b

THE PIVOT

Assume starting position.

a Keep the left hand on the floor, right hand on the right ankle. Raise the left leg up in back and hold in that position. Lift the right heel and turn it to the left and the right 10 times, pivoting on the toes. Reverse leg positions and pivot 10 times on the left foot. Gradually work up to 20 times with each foot.

b Stand. Rest for 10 counts. Then bend the left knee. Place the right hand on the floor. Grasp the right ankle with the left hand. Slowly lower the right knee as close to the floor as possible. Then try to straighten the left leg. Repeat 5 times with each leg.

Starting position

a

b

DOUBLE PIVOT

Assume starting position.

   a   Lean torso over bent right knee. Turn
both heels side to side, pivoting on the balls
of the feet. At the same time, swing the arms
side to side at knee level. Repeat for 5 counts.

   b   Bend lower and continue pivoting
heels, swinging the arms at the ankle level, for
5 counts. Repeat (5 counts at knee level,
5 counts at ankle level) 10 times over the right
knee, 10 times over the left knee.

Starting position

a

THE ARCH

Assume starting position.

a Swing the left leg forward and up to the side as high as possible.

b Continue bringing the leg forward to touch the floor in front. Do this in one continuous movement, forming an imaginary arch with the leg. Then swing the leg in an arch back to the starting position. Swing forward and back 10 times with each leg.

Starting position

a

DADDY LONG LEGS

Assume Starting Position.

    a Keep the left hand on the left ankle. Lift the right leg up from the side to meet the left leg.

    b Lower the right leg directly forward to the floor. Lift right leg straight up again. Then return the leg to the floor directly to the side. Repeat (up, forward, up, side) 10 times with each leg.

Starting position

a

COOL DOWN CHAIR CHAMPS I

Assume starting position.

   a Keep hands on the seat of the chair.
Lift the left leg to hip height. Swing the leg
forward to the side, then back. Repeat 15 times
with each leg.

   b Place the right foot on the seat of the
chair. Turn the toes out to the side, so that the
outer edge of the foot rests on the chair. Bend
the left knee. Slowly reach hands to the right
ankle. Hold for 5 counts. Do once with each leg.

Starting position

a

COOL DOWN   CHAIR CHAMPS II

Assume starting position.

a Keep the right forearm on the seat of the chair, left hand gripping the chair. Move the left leg in large circles to the side 15 times. Then place the left forearm on the chair and circle the right leg 15 times.

b Place the left foot on top of the back of the chair. Bend the right knee to grasp the back of the chair. Slowly bend the right knee further down, then up, 5 times. Reverse leg positions and bounce 5 times with the left knee.

*Starting
position*

a

b

WARM UP THE CHARLESTON I

Assume starting position.

a Hop on the right foot, kicking the left leg across to the right. At the same time, swing the arms to the left. Jump, feet together. Then hop on the left foot, kicking the right leg across to the left, swinging the arms to the right. Return to jump in center. Repeat 10 times.

b Place feet together, knees bent. Open the knees, extending arms out to the sides. Then close the knees, crossing the arms above the knees. Repeat 5 times.

Starting position

a

b

WARM UP THE CHARLESTON II

Assume starting position.

a Hop on the right foot, kicking the left foot up behind the right. Touch the foot with the right hand. Jump, feet together. Then hop on the left foot, kicking the right foot up behind the left. Touch the right foot with the left hand. Return to jump in the center. Repeat 10 times.

b Place the hands on the hips. Raise the shoulders. Shake the right leg for 5 counts. Then shake the left leg for 5 counts.

Starting position

a

REACH OUT

Assume starting position.

a Press the right heel down, straightening the right leg. Reach the right arm straight forward. At the same time, bend the left knee, lift the left heel, and pull the left elbow back. Alternately lift heels, switching arm positions 30 times. (If your back is weak, do not lean forward. Do the exercise upright.)

b Kneel, hands on the floor, head down. Round the back by pulling up on the abdominal muscles. Hold for 5 counts. Then slowly flatten the back. Hold for 5 counts. Round and flatten the back 3 times.

Starting position

a

CIRCLE & KICK MAGIC

Assume starting position.

a Bending from the waist, swing the right arm forward and up.

b Continue circling the arm up overhead and back.

c On the back swing, lean back to place the right hand on the floor. Lift the left leg as high as possible, touching the ankle with the left hand. Return to starting position. Repeat 15 times with each leg.

Starting position

a

b

HAMSTRING STRETCH

Assume starting position.

    a Keep left hand on the floor under the right knee, right toes up, right hand on the knee to support the back. Bend the left elbow down to the floor. Then straighten the elbow. Repeat 10 times. Reverse arm and leg positions and repeat with the right elbow 10 times.

    b In the starting position, place the right foot flat on the floor. Place the left hand on the floor behind the right heel. Bend the left elbow to the floor and straighten 10 times. Reverse arm and leg positions and repeat with the right elbow 10 times.

*Starting
position*

a

HIP LIFTER

Assume starting position.

a Raise both legs straight up from the side.

b Then lower legs forward to the floor. Lift legs up again. Then return to the floor at the side. Repeat 5 times to the right side, 5 times to the left side. Work up to 10 times each side.

c Sit, right leg straight forward on the floor. Cross the left foot to the floor outside the right knee. Grasp the left ankle with both hands. Pull the head down toward the ankle. Hold for 5 counts. Do once with each foot.

Starting position

a

b

SWEEP UP

Assume starting position.

a Lift the hips off the floor, shifting the weight to the right hand and knee. Swing the left arm forward at the same time.

b Continue the motion, lifting hips higher, extending the left leg straight back, swinging the left arm up. Then swing back down to the starting position. Repeat 10 times to each side.

Starting position

a

b

COOL DOWN   THE TABLE

Assume starting position.

a   Lift the right leg and bend the knee in toward the chest. Then kick the leg straight up.

b   Bend the knee in toward the chest again. Then kick the leg straight forward. Repeat (knee in, kick up, knee in, kick forward) 15 times with each leg.

*Starting
position*

a

COOL DOWN   JUMPING BEAN

Assume starting position.

a   Jump up and down, keeping knees slightly bent. Land lightly on the feet. Jump 20 times. Work up to 30 times.

b   Place the right leg forward, knee bent, in a lunge position. Extend the left leg back. Turn the right foot to the side. Clasp the right ankle with both hands. Slowly straighten the right leg. Bend and straighten the leg 5 times. Reverse leg positions and repeat 5 times with the left leg.

113

Starting position

a

WARM UP   THE DANCER

Assume starting position.

   a Hop on the left foot, lifting the right knee up to the side, turning torso to the right. At the same time, swing both arms to the left.

   b Hop on the left foot again, returning the right foot to the floor. At the same time, turn torso to the left, swinging arms to the right. Repeat 10 times with each leg.

   c Bend the right knee up toward the chest. Hold the bottom of the foot with both hands. Slowly straighten the leg as much as possible. Hold for 5 counts. Lower foot to the floor. Do once with each leg.

115

Starting position

a

WARM UP   KEEP DANCING

Assume starting position.

a   Step to the right and leap on the right foot, landing with right knee bent. On the leap, swing the arms up to the right and extend the left leg up to the side. Then step to the left and leap on the left foot, swinging arms up to the left, right leg up to the side. Leap right then left 10 times.

b   Stand with the feet together. Bend the knees. Place the hands on the floor outside the feet, fingers turned back.

c   Very slowly try to straighten the legs, keeping the hands flat on the floor. Hold for 5 counts. Relax. Then slowly uncurl the back and return to an upright position. (If you have a weak back, do not straighten the knees completely. Straighten only until you feel a pull in the back of the legs.)

*Starting
position*

a

FIGURE SHAPER I

Assume starting position.

a Bending the right knee slightly, cross the left leg behind the right, touching foot to the floor. At the same time, swing the arms down and across to the right. Return to starting position. Repeat 10 times with each leg.

b Cross the left leg behind the right. Place both hands on the right knee. Bend and straighten the right leg 5 times. Then reverse leg positions and repeat 5 times with the left leg.

119

Starting position

a

b

FIGURE SHAPER II

Assume starting position.

a   Bending the right knee slightly, cross the left leg behind the right, touching the foot to the floor. At the same time, swing the hands down to touch the ankles. Return to starting position. Repeat 10 times with each leg.

b   Cross the left leg behind the right. Hold the ankles. Slowly try to straighten both legs in a long stretch. Hold for 5 counts. Then reverse leg positions and repeat the stretch. Do once with each leg.

Starting position

a

UP, UP, AND AWAY

Assume starting position.

 a Shifting the weight to the right hand and knee, lift the torso. Swing the left arm forward and up, lifting the left leg straight back.

 b Then place both hands on the floor, bending the elbows. Lift the left leg up in back as high as possible. Return to starting position. Repeat 10 times with each leg. Try to flow in this exercise, going from the starting position to the leg lift in one smooth motion.

Starting position

a

CIRCLE SWEEP

Assume starting position.

a With weight on the right hand and knee, lift the torso. Bring the left knee and left arm forward.

b Extend the leg up to the side. Swing the arm to the side to follow the motion of the leg.

c Swing the leg and arm straight back. Return to starting position. Repeat 10 times with each leg. Try to do this exercise in one smooth motion. Form an imaginary circle as the arm and leg move forward, side, back, and down to the starting position.

Starting position

a

COOL DOWN RAGTIME REVIVER

Assume starting position.

a Hop on the right foot, bending the left knee to cross the left leg up behind the right. At the same time, swing arms to the right. Then jump, feet together.

b Hop on the left foot, bending the right knee to cross the right leg up behind the left. Swing arms to the left. Return to jump in the center. Kick up left leg then right leg 30 times.

Starting position

COOL DOWN   ENERGY BOOSTER

Assume starting position.

a Lift knees in an easy run-in-place for 30 counts. Gradually increase the counts as you build up strength.

b Stand with the feet wide apart. Extend the right arm up. Grasp the elbow with the left hand. Pull the right arm across to the left. Stretch for 5 counts. Do once with each arm.